TIME and TIDE
An Atlas for the Grieving

Denise Thompson-Slaughter

Copyright © 2021 Denise Thompson-Slaughter. All rights reserved under International and Pan-American Copyright Conventions. No part of this book may be reproduced or distributed in any form or by any means, or stored in a data base or retrieval system, without written permission from the author. All rights reserved.

ISBN: 978-1-63210-087-0

Acknowledgments

"Lament" and "My Ghosts" were first published by *Nine Cloud Journal* online (August 2020).
"Mourning Tote" and "A Theft of Crutches Leaves Everyone Lame" were first published by *Tipton Poetry Journal* (Summer 2020).
"The New Normal" was first published in Bill Memmet's column in *The* [Rochester, NY] *Democrat & Chronicle* on October 23, 2020.
Thanks also go to Ann Finger and Peggy Weston Byrd for their reading, good advice, and encouragement.

Plain View Press   http://plainviewpress.net
1101 W. 34th Street, STE 404, Austin, TX 78705

Dedicated to the Grieving

*with special thanks to the medical personnel
and first responders during
the Covid-19 pandemic*

*This is time for us. Memory and nostalgia. The pain of absence.
But it isn't absence that causes sorrow. It is affection and love.*

—Carlo Rovelli, The Order of Time

CONTENTS

Against the Tide	7
Whys and Wherefores	8
The Answers Are at the End	9
Dream from Raindrop Lake	10
Covid 19–20, New York City	11
Pandemic Haiku	12
The Purell Bottle Is Half Full	13
The Quick & the Dead	14
A Theft of Crutches Leaves Everyone Lame	15
The New Normal	16
Mourning Tote	17
My Ghosts	18
"It Could Have Been Worse"	19
A Nation's Women Mourn	20
Murder of an Innocent	21
The Club No One Wants to Belong To	22
Where Does It End?	23
2020	25
Lament	27
Personal Protective Prisons	28
The Clearing	29

Against the Tide

At the spot where the land took you,
I hang on to the pier,
arms wrapped tight around a wooden pylon
connecting earth to the river of time.

I will not go, I say.
I will not leave the spot where you disappeared.
Surely you have not gone far
and someday I may glimpse you through the trees
or collecting shiny quartz along the shore.

The water keeps on gurgling around me
and for a while, time stops.
Months go by and I scarcely move, scarcely think,
take marathon naps with the wooden post for my pillow.

Barnacles begin to cling, but I don't care:
I sense you near at times, hear your voice, feel your presence.
Sometimes I know you've given me a hug or
told me to stop crying and sleep.
I see you in my dreams, but you are always walking
away from me
or deflating like a balloon from the tremendous
expenditure of energy that's required to stay near.
I know you have work to do and must travel to higher ground,
but it is hard to let you go.

Eventually the spring floods come.
The raucous river is full of new water, new life, new eddies and
sites of interest, even to me.
My grip loosens and the waves pull me from my post,
wash me further downstream
with my hands full of splinters,
bobbing like a cork,
anchorless.

Whys and Wherefores

Why are you not here to talk about the race for President?
Why are you not here to massage my shoulders when I'm tense
or ask me how I feel or how I slept?
And where are your hugs?
Why are you not here to discuss the news or metaphysics,
to critique our parenting,
carry our boxes up and down the stairs?
Why are you not here to play with the dog,
to spend quality time with the cat,
to help trim the bushes?
Why are you not here to drink all the juice—
do you want it to go to waste?

Where are you when it thunders and I worry you're afraid but
just too grown up to admit it?
Where are you when I want to comfort you
or think I should make eggs the way *you* like them?
Why are you not here to watch the Superbowl with your poor
brokenhearted father?
And where are you when it's time to celebrate your birthday,
fill your Easter basket or
your Christmas stocking?
Do they even *have* Peeps or Rice Krispy Treats in that other
    so-called dimension?

The Answers Are at the End

We humans like meaning with our meaty lives.
We see patterns in the carpet,
faces in the knotty pine,
we project pictures on the starry sky.
We're always connecting the dots.

We ask why, why, why
until any god who exists
must tire of our whining and our
tiresome toddler questions.
Is the universe deaf and indifferent, or
are we simply too small to understand the answers?

Dream from Raindrop Lake
(after the death of a son)

The raindrops silver up the leaves, filigreed beads
on a hosta's gown,
while I remind myself that life
is but a dream,
one entering its final REM stage, I hope,
because I am oh so tired of
row row rowing my boat.

I used to feel proud to be a survivor of,
well, so many things.
They seemed like big things at the time.
In my naïve pride I had no idea
how tough life could get.

Don't let your victories go to your head—
in this game, each level gets harder, and,
although you may get more rest between challenges,
you'll need it.

Drink deep of delta sleep.
You never know when your little boat
in the silver raindrop lake
may float you into the lead role
in the Book of Job.

Covid 19–20, New York City

Even more than most queues in the city,
the line moves slowly to enter Elmhurst Hospital for a swab test.
Too often when a bed clears,
the former occupant is carried to the refrigerated truck out back.

The truck attendee in his mask, gloves, and coverall is spooked,
surrounded by so many rising souls, their carapaces below
with lungs glued shut by a microscopic microbial foe.

The ones who may survive continue to rest in their beds,
attended by exhausted nurses and other heroes who
must make do with improvised equipment, insufficient supplies,
and too few donations from the federal government of
ventilators that turn out to be past their expiration date.

The governor pleads for more help,
warns that the city is the proverbial canary in the coal mine.
Makers of bespoke suits, renowned among politicians and
businessmen everywhere,
retool in Rochester to make protective masks.
Automakers evolve to produce ventilators.

Congress argues on, politicians too alienated from one another
to iron out the details of a relief package
until weeks into the crisis when
New York has already lost the first five hundred voters.
There will be tens of thousands more.

Pandemic Haiku

(1)

Amid spring flowers,
unattended funerals.
Mourners go unhugged.

(2)

We all brim with tears,
each mourning cumulative,
past losses relived.

The Purell Bottle Is Half Full

Sometimes it helps to think that
our loved ones have been spared *worse* things.

Dad died six months before 9/11—
which would surely have brought on the massive stroke
if he hadn't already had it.

My dear son, sweet and distracted mess that he was,
would never have remembered to wash his hands often enough
to keep from getting Covid and spreading it to us,
with perhaps disastrous consequences that
would have crushed him with guilt.

In such times can death be kind?
Can death be timely?
Is it all meaningless—or can love provide
an umbrella of grace?

How lucky were those who died of old age right before
the Black Plague?
Those who had heart attacks in Nagasaki the day before
the bomb fell?

The Quick & the Dead

When your dead outnumber your quick
and you can't imagine what's left to do,
you perhaps will know this fancy to be true:
Time is a slippery eel of delusion
and there's a temporal illusion and a place for everything—
including you.

And you will wait to discover *why* you must wait,
sometimes with forced gaiety,
sometimes just sleeping or seeking whatever harmless
or helpful thing will cause the days to slither past.
Maybe this time will be good, kind,
free of physical pain—
or maybe not.

When finally your ship arrives, heralded
by the parting of the angels, eels, or other creatures
of the high and low dimensions,
you will embark with relief, then
call *adieu* and *amore*,
bestowing blessings on all those left on shore
 as they strain to see you beyond the growing mist.
They are trapped in time and cannot perceive you.

You can see everything.

A Theft of Crutches Leaves Everyone Lame

Mark Twain's greatest regret
was that he'd convinced his wife
there was no afterlife.

Later, when she lay dying in grievous pain,
he could see what he'd done:
robbed her of hope and comfort
in her last days.

That deathbed stare: despair!
The only unforgiveable sin, supposedly,
is that against the Holy Ghost.

Neither, Twain found, could he forgive himself.

The New Normal

Children ride by on bikes, hailing one another from afar.
Rakes hiss and scrape dead leaves out of brown wintered beds.
It all sounds like normal spring
until you remember why so many people are at home.

We enjoy sunny walks but must cross the street
when someone walks toward us.
Go ahead and stroll in the street—
there's no traffic! How bizarre.

It's not war, not earthquake
nor environmental catastrophe
with rising seas or poison air.
It's just a normal plague month in spring.

Mourning Tote

Mourning comes, the darkness stays.
We think of all the thousand ways
we're fragile and prone to mistake,
while others we for granted take.

We counted on those who cut our hair,
who made us smile, who loved to share,
who treated our pets and our maladies
in better times, by far, than these.

We dream of those whom we have lost
and watch the rose poke through the frost.
The year advances as it will,
but we tote up our losses still.

My Ghosts

I am quarantined at home with my many ghosts.
They are kind and quiet and sometimes comforting.
But they do like that one chair in the bedroom and
often leave the spot quite cold.
They need to suck out the heat
to make their presence felt on such a lowly level as ours.
It's difficult for them, I think,
so I'm grateful for their company.

Probably they want me to meditate,
perhaps pray with real focus, to meet them partway.
It's a hard ask in such anxious times
to blank my mind or sit straight, all aligned.

If they're waiting for me to join them,
they'll just have to wait
until after Election Day.
The afterlife may be sweet,
but I have a duty to meet—
and months to go before I sleep.

"It Could Have Been Worse"

It could have been Ebola
or the Black Plague or the Red Death,
something bodily gross, bloody.
It could have lasted a decade.
Thirteen times as many could have died.

It could have started in December,
cancelling imminent holidays,
preparations already made,
and the long winter still ahead of us.
We could have lost heat, electricity, water—
internet!
We could have been ground zero, with zero warning, like China.

It could have left survivors sterile, deaf, blind, or deranged.
It could have taken all the children.
It could have left us starving, rather than eyeing the dubious
expired cans and boxes in the back of the pantry.
It could have left us instead to speculate on all the creatures
that *might* really taste like chicken.

It could have released the Beast in humankind,
turned the spoiled, stubborn, and whiny species we've become
into something more monstrous.
It could have been worse.

But then again, it could have been better.

A Nation's Women Mourn

Fighting through the pain
to lead the people to safety,
she almost made it.

Relentless
Unstoppable
Truth warrior
Honorable
RBG

Murder of an Innocent

Breonna, Breonna,
queen of the year's unjustly dead.
The Louisville cops after midnight
smashed the door and woke her from bed.

No drugs, no drug dealers,
no felon they searched for were found;
her boyfriend tried to protect her
but she ended up dead on the ground.

Five times the men shot her—
she bled out on the floor.
This young EMT couldn't save herself
from the white men at her door.

Her friend begged them for medics
but they put off making the call;
they took him out and arrested *him;*
Breonna Taylor had no chance at all.

It appears there will be no justice.
The fix is most definitely in.
Every daughter's mother is heartbroken
Because Breonna's murder's a sin.

The Club No One Wants to Belong To

A parent's loss of a child—
raised for years, loved, molded, and sacrificed for—
has no measure.
Whether robbed by disease, suicide, accident, or violence,
all of us dwell in rooms of earthly hell
with only paper-thin walls between us,
our nerve endings raw and invisibly twitching.

Mothers, fathers, sisters, brothers, others,
I grieve with you.
Don't you get sick of everyone saying
"I don't know how you do it"?
There is no how.
There is only to die or to keep breathing,
to let life drag you through the bright, brittle days,
the achingly heartbroken nights.

Don't you want to smack the ones who
tell you you'll feel better with time
or who question the level of faith your child had?—
as if any God worth knowing would ever turn away
your baby, regardless of age or belief.
Don't you want to throw yourself into walls sometimes?
Jump in an industrial dryer and let it pound the
pain out of your body?
Don't you want a time machine?
A superpower to save lives?

But the only superpower you've got
is putting one foot in front of the other.
So,
we do it again today.

Where Does It End?
(for Daniel Prude)

The big man whose mind had broken down again
was forced to lie naked on an icy street on his stomach
for some time before they covered his head and
crushed the air out of him.

No blanket, no ambulance until it was too late,
no compassion for his illness, his suffering.
Who acts like this? Not someone *less* broken.

Although he was peacefully pliant to their every command,
the police got scared when he eventually started to squirm
and make distressing sounds and maybe spit.
Think about his private parts being pressed into the ice.
Squirm much?

At least three neurally-different young men
were attacked by police this year.
The white 12-year-old survived—but at what cost to an
already fragile mind?

One out of ten people suffers a major mental illness
at some time in their life.
Hitler planned to kill them all.
Is that where we're going?

It could have happened to someone you know.
It could have happened to my child.
It could happen to yours.

When fear turns into hate, there's no telling
where it will lead.
When difference inspires that old multiplier, fear,
more and more of us begin to look "different."

It is time for compassion and courage.
It is time to befriend the stranger.
It is time to stop fearing difference.
It is past time for a change.

2020

Year from hell broken open,
1918, 1929, and 1968 rolled into one
with unprecedented new horrors on top.

The numerals looked so round and pleasant,
like a date from "The Jetsons" TV show—
simple, clean, easy.
Instead it brought the people
    brain-eating amoebas in the water supply
    cover-ups
    death of the righteous
    depression
    derecho
    dictators
    disease
    division
    double hurricanes
    economic crash
    explosions
    fires
    floods
    joblessness
    heat rays
    liars in high places
    loss of relatives
    massacres
    murder hornets
    nazis
    no hope
    no justice
    no peace
    no one taking responsibility

pandemic
paranoia
pepper balls
protests
riots
state-sponsored killing
tear gas
threats
tornadoes
zombie storms.
Could it get any worse? Don't ask!

Lament

Imagine
death without rituals,
grief without hugs,
mourning without companionship,
comfort without community.
You *can* imagine
because it's here.

Saturn, King of Karma, the Lord's bad cop,
brings all the chickens home to roost
at the end of his saturnine cycle.
What will we learn
to take forward into the new beginning?
Will we?

Personal Protective Prisons

Climb Maslow's pyramid of needs—
come face to face with the fact
that we are all prisoners of our own bodies,
locked into the prisms of our minds.

We love through a glass darkly,
converge, merge for but a moment of joy,
diverge again into our own crystal neuro-forests.
But oh how we long for that moment
when the glass blocks melt!

The Clearing
2021

We learn again what it is like
to be grateful for each sunny day,
each friendly voice or
electronic remembrance.

We have taken too much for granted,
have gotten lost in the forest
without taking time to see the trees,
to measure how far we've come—and how fast.

Blinded by the bright light of our
daily scavenger hunts,
constantly seeking the next thing,
we cannot be accused of nostalgia.

But when the world changes,
we again recall our intricate roots,
remember our forebearers and our growth,
take time to honor those many we have lost.

The day has come, in this forest glade
to simply appreciate the living of life.

www.ingramcontent.com/pod-product-compliance
Lightning Source LLC
Chambersburg PA
CBHW070242090526
44586CB00036B/2131